Plants

Written by Sally Hewitt

W

First published in 2010 by Franklin Watts
338 Euston Road, London NW1 3BH

Franklin Watts Australia
Level 17/207 Kent Street, Sydney NSW 2000

Editor: Katie Dicker
Art Direction: Rahul Dhiman (Q2AMedia)
Designer: Shruti Aggarwal (Q2AMedia)
Picture researcher: Ekta Sharma (Q2AMedia)
Craft models made by: Divij Singh (Q2AMedia)
Photography: Divij Singh (Q2AMedia)

Picture credits:
t=top b=bottom c=centre l=left r=right

Cover: Photostogo, Shutterstock
Title page: Misscanon/Dreamstime.
Insides: Andrzej Tokarski/Dreamstime: 4c, Shutterstock:4b,
Antonio Jorge Nunes/Shutterstock: 6, Craig Hanson/
Shutterstock: 7t, Nancy Nehring/Istockphoto: 7b, Gabriele
Meermann/Photolibrary: 8t, Misscanon/Dreamstime: 8b,
Sheldon Levis/Photolibrary: 10t, Richard Gleed/
Photolibrary: 10b, Shutterstock: 11t, Shutterstock: 11cl,
Andrzej Tokarski/Dreamstime: 11cr, Silver-John/
Shutterstock: 12t, Leroy Alfonse/Photolibrary: 12b,
Kapoen/Shutterstock: 14b, Oliver Hoffmann/Shutterstock:
16t, Richard Griffin/123RF: 16b, Robert Maass/Corbis: 18t,
Elenamiv/Shutterstock: 18b, Vishnevskiy
Vasily/Shutterstock: 20t, Brian A Jackson/Shutterstock:
20b, Alina Solovyova-Vincent/Istockphoto: 21cl, Kristian
Sekulic/Shutterstock: 21cr, Mike Norton/Shutterstock: 22,
Paul Harris/Photolibrary: 23t, Masterfile: 24b, Elena
Schweitzer/Shutterstock: 25t, Intraclique LLC/Shutterstock:
25c, Joellen L Armstrong/Shutterstock: 25br, Nicole S.
Young/Istockphoto: 25bl, Bart Sadowski/Istockphoto: 26t,
Frances M Roberts/Photolibrary: 26b.
Q2AMedia Image Bank: Contents page, 9, 11t, 13, 15,
17, 19, 21t.
Q2AMedia Art Bank: 9, 14, 17, 23, 24, 27.

With thanks to our model Shruti Aggarwal.

A CIP catalogue record for this book
is available from the British Library.

ISBN: 978 0 7496 8761 8

Dewey Classification: 580'22

Printed in China

Franklin Watts is a division of Hachette Children's
Books, an Hachette UK company.
www.hachette.co.uk

Contents

Words that appear in **bold** can be found in the glossary on pages 28–29.

What is a plant?

Plants are alive. Like all living things, they need food and water to live and grow. But unlike other living things, they make their own food. Plants use air, water and a green **pigment** in their leaves, called **chlorophyll**, to make food from sunlight.

Plants for life

Plants grow all over planet Earth. Life on Earth couldn't exist without plants. They provide food for animals and people. They help to keep the air full of the **oxygen** we breathe. Plants are also part of the **water cycle** because they absorb (take in) water and release it into the air as a gas called **water vapour**.

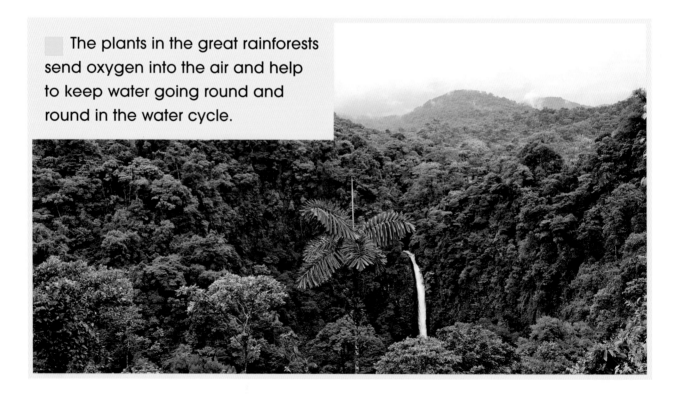

The plants in the great rainforests send oxygen into the air and help to keep water going round and round in the water cycle.

Flowering plants

Most plants are flowering plants. The flower is the part of the plant where **fruit** and **seeds** are made. New plants grow from the seeds. Flowering plants are all shapes and sizes. A big horse chestnut tree is a type of flowering plant, and so is a tiny daisy and a prickly cactus.

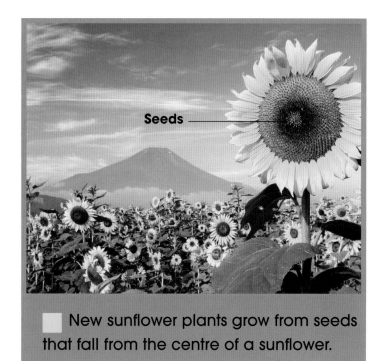

Seeds

New sunflower plants grow from seeds that fall from the centre of a sunflower.

Non-flowering plants

Plants that don't produce flowers are called non-flowering plants. Seaweed is a type of non-flowering plant that grows in sea water. Moss is a non-flowering plant that grows on logs and walls. They make new plants from **spores** instead of seeds. Their spores look like tiny specks of dust.

Ferns are a type of non-flowering plant. The brown clusters on this fern hold its spores.

Parts of a plant

Flowering plants all have roots, a stem, leaves and flowers. Roots take in water and hold the plant in place, the stem supports the plant, green leaves make food for the plant and the flower is where seeds are formed.

Drinking in water

Water and **minerals** from the soil are sucked up through the plant's roots and carried along tubes in the roots, stem and leaves. The veins you see on leaves carry this water and food. Roots and leaves have a skin that keeps in water. Some water vapour escapes through tiny holes in the leaves.

Flower

Leaf

Stem

Roots

All parts of a plant need to be healthy for it to grow well.

All these different plants have roots, stems, leaves and flowers.

Different plants

Plants **adapt** to survive where they live. Daisies have thin, fine roots that hold the plants in place in shallow soil. Trees have a woody stem to hold them upright. Ivy stems bend and curl up walls, fences and other plants for support.

Watch water go through a plant

You will need:
- 3 jars of water • blue food colouring • old carrot
- celery stalk with leaves
- white carnation • paper and crayons (or a camera)

1 Put enough drops of food colouring in each jar to make the water a strong blue colour.

2 Put the carrot, the celery stalk and the carnation in the jars.

3 Draw the plant in each jar, copying the colours as accurately as you can (or take a photograph).

4 Look at the jars every few hours during the day and again the next day. Draw or photograph the changes you see. Record your findings on a chart.

	Carrot (root)	Celery (stalk and leaves)	Carnation (flower)	Comments
2 hours	✗✗✗	blue lines starting to show at the bottom of the celery stalk	✗✗✗	✗✗✗
8 hours		✗✗✗	✗✗✗	✗✗✗
24 hours	✗✗✗	✗✗✗		✗✗✗

Does the carrot, the celery or the flower look the most blue at the end of your experiment? How quickly do the changes occur? Why do you think this is?

What do plants need?

Plants need sunlight, air, water and minerals to grow. With a good supply of all these things, a plant should grow well. If a plant does not grow well, it is probably not getting enough of at least one of them.

Sunlight

Plants need sunlight because they use **energy** from the Sun to make food in their leaves. In a rainforest, the leaves and branches of tall trees block out the sunlight. Smaller plants grow high up on the branches of the trees so that they can get enough sunlight.

These orchids are growing on a tree trunk to reach the sunlight.

Indoor plants need to be watered and fed with minerals.

Soil and water

Plants are mostly made of water, so they need water to grow. They also need minerals from the soil. Indoor pot plants need plant food (with minerals) to stay healthy. Too much water can make plants rot and wilt, but without enough water, they dry out and die.

Watch seedlings grow

Geranium seedlings will work well in this activity

You will need:
- 4 seedlings • potting soil
- 3 small flower pots • small watering can • jar of water
- ruler or tape measure

1 Give the first seedling all it needs to grow. Plant it in soil, put it in a sunny place and give it enough water to keep the soil moist.

2 Plant the second seedling, keep it watered but put it in a dark cupboard. Plant the third seedling, put it in a sunny place but don't water it. Put the fourth seedling in a jar of water in a sunny place.

3 Keep a record of how each seedling grows. Write your findings down on a chart.

Seedling	Day	Height	Comments
1 – soil, water, sunlight	2	6 cm	taller and healthy looking
	5	6.5 cm	2 new leaves
	8	×××	×××
2 – soil, water, no sunlight	2	5 cm	looking a bit pale
	5	×××	×××
	8	×××	×××
3 – soil, no water, sunlight	2	5 cm	wilting slightly

Which seedling grows the best? Which seedling grows the worst? What conditions do the seedlings prefer? Why do you think that is? You could repeat this experiment with seedlings of a different plant. Remember to wash your hands after you touch soil.

Making food

Plants make food in their leaves. Their leaves have to be the best shape and size to catch sunlight. Broadleaf trees, such as maple and oak, have thin leaves with a large surface area to catch as much sunlight as possible.

Photosynthesis

Photosynthesis is the way that plants make their own food. Sunlight is absorbed by the chlorophyll in their leaves. Energy from sunlight is used to turn water and **carbon dioxide** from the air into food.

Sunlight helps plants to make food in their leaves, to give them the energy to grow.

The leaves of this plant have turned yellow from lack of sunlight.

Green and growing

When plants with green leaves cannot get sunlight, they start to turn yellow and droop. There is less chlorophyll in their leaves because they cannot make enough food. When the Sun shines on the plant again, its chlorophyll levels rise and the leaves turn green again.

Make some leaf stencils

You will need:
- healthy houseplant with large green leaves • card
- scissors • poster putty
- small watering can

1 Cut out pairs of card shapes smaller than the leaves, such as stars, diamonds and circles.

2 Use the poster putty to stick one shape on top of a leaf and the other directly below it on the underside of the leaf. Repeat with the other shapes on different leaves.

4 Leave the plant in a sunny position and water it. After about a week, check under the card shapes to see if the leaves have started to turn yellow.

How long does it take for the leaves under the card shapes to turn yellow?

How long does it take for the leaves to turn green again when the card shapes are removed?

Flowers

Flowers contain the parts a plant needs to make seeds. Some seeds grow into new plants. Seeds form after **pollination** has taken place.

Pollination

During pollination, **pollen** is carried by the wind or animals from the stamens (the male part of the flower) to the pistil (the female part). When a pollen grain reaches the **ovary**, seeds start to form. Seeds contain everything needed for a new plant to grow. Pollination usually takes place between plants. Some plants are **self-pollinated**.

Petal

Pollen

Stamen

Pistil

Ovary

Most flowers have these parts, which are used for pollination.

An insect looking for nectar to drink carries pollen from flower to flower.

Attracting insects

Some flowers have brightly coloured and scented petals. They attract insects that drink a sweet juice called **nectar** from the centre of the flower. As the insect drinks, pollen sticks to its legs and body. It carries the pollen on to the next flower.

Discover the parts of a flower

You will need:
- big flower with colourful, scented petals • white card • clear glue or clear sticky-backed plastic
- pencil or pen

Hibiscus flower

1 Carefully pull each petal off the flower. Count the petals and lay them out on the white card.

2 Pull off each stamen. Count them and lay them out on the card.

3 Remove the pistil and the ovary without separating them.

4 Write the name of the flower and label the parts.

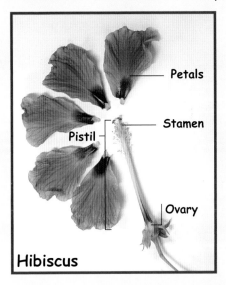

Petals

Stamen

Pistil

Ovary

Hibiscus

5 Cover the whole card with the sticky-backed plastic or spread glue on the card and lay the parts on top. You could also press a whole flower to include in your display.

Petals
Stamen
Pistil
Ovary
Hibiscus

Do this with several different types of flower. Compare the number of petals and stamens, the size and colour of the petals and anything else you notice.

Germination

When a flower has done its job, it dies. Then the ovary swells and becomes the fruit that contains the seeds. The way a new plant starts to grow from a seed is called **germination**.

Finding seeds

Some fruits have seeds inside them. An avocado pear has one big seed inside it and an apple has several little pips. Other fruits carry seeds on the outside. You can see seeds on a strawberry's skin and stripy seeds packed together on a sunflower head.

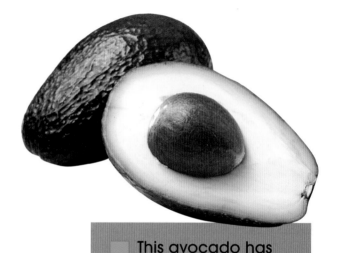

This avocado has a big seed in its centre.

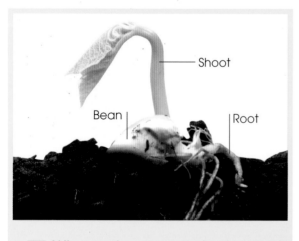

Shoot

Bean

Root

When a bean germinates, the shoot grows up towards the light.

Growing seeds

Inside a seed (or a bean) is a tiny root and a shoot. The seed also has a store of food to feed the plant until it grows leaves and can make food of its own. To germinate, all seeds need water, oxygen and the right temperature. Some seeds need darkness and others need light.

Grow beans in a jar

You will need:
- large, flat beans such as broad beans (or fava beans) • glass jar • kitchen towel (or cotton wool)
- paper • ruler
- pencil and crayons

1 Soak a few beans in water overnight.

2 Damp some kitchen towel right through with water. Use it to line the jar.

3 Push the beans equal distances apart in between the jar and the damp kitchen towel.

4 Leave the jar somewhere warm and light and make sure the kitchen towel is always damp.

Keep a record of each new plant's growth. You could draw pictures, write comments and take measurements. Plant the seedlings in pots of soil when they start to grow leaves.

Day	Picture of growth	Root/shoot measurement
1		0 cm
4		2 cm
7		Root 3.5 cm/ shoot 1 cm

Bulbs and tubers

Some plants have **bulbs** or **tubers** that are underground food stores. Each year, a new plant grows from the bulb or tuber. The baby plant uses this store of food to grow.

Bulbs

Onions, tulips, daffodils and lilies are all plants that grow from bulbs. Bulbs are made up of layers of thick leaves storing food that surround a new plant waiting to grow. During the cold winter, a bulb rests under the soil. The new plant starts to grow in spring when it gets warmer.

Bulbs planted in the autumn will begin to grow in the spring.

Shoots

A potato starts to shrivel as growing shoots use up the food it has stored.

Roots and tubers

Some plants store food made by photosynthesis during the summer in their roots and stems. A carrot is a root swollen with stored food and a potato is a swollen underground stem called a tuber. In the spring, shoots and new roots start to grow.

Grow some new plants

Ask an adult to help you with this activity

You will need:
- flower pot of soil
- onion • carrot
- saucer of water
- 4 toothpicks • sweet potato
- jar of water

Carrot

Sweet potato — Onion roots

Onion

1 Plant an onion in the flower pot, with the roots facing downwards. Cover it in soil.

2 Ask an adult to slice the top off a carrot. Place the carrot top in a saucer of water.

3 Push four toothpicks into the sweet potato. Use the toothpicks to hang the potato in the top of the jar so the bottom of it is in the water.

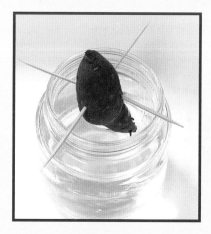

4 Keep the soil damp in the flower pot, and the saucer filled with water. Make sure part of the sweet potato is always in the water.

5 Be patient over a few weeks and the bulb, the root and the tuber will all start to grow. Keep a diary of your growing plants.

Spreading seeds

Plants produce a lot of seeds because only a few seeds will find a good place to grow. Plants have many different ways of spreading their seeds to give them a good chance of starting new life.

Animals

Fruit, seeds and nuts are all eaten by animals. When birds eat berries and fly away, the seeds later fall to the ground in their droppings. Squirrels bury nuts in the ground to eat later and then forget where some are. The 'planted' nuts start to grow into new trees.

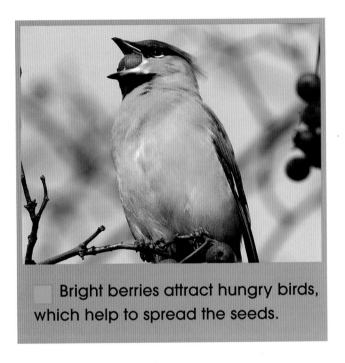
Bright berries attract hungry birds, which help to spread the seeds.

Dandelion seeds hang from parachutes that blow in the wind.

Hooks and wings

Hooks, wings and explosions are some of the other ways that seeds spread. Seeds called hitchhikers catch onto clothes or animal fur. Maple seeds whirl through the air on wings. Cranesbill seedpods explode!

Discover some hidden seeds

You will need:
- 3 seed trays
- trowel
- small watering can
- card
- pencil

Under the sycamore tree, 3 April

1 Collect soil from three different locations, such as under a sycamore tree, by a sunny wall, and next to a rose bush.

2 Put the soil in the seed trays. Label where the soil came from and the date. Water the soil lightly and keep the trays watered in a warm, light place.

3 Write down which plants were growing in each location. Write down which plants you think might grow from seeds hiding in the soil. For example, a sycamore tree because there is one nearby, or dandelions because there is uncut grass nearby.

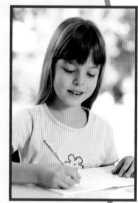

4 When plants start to grow in the seed trays, identify them using a field guide or the Internet. You could also compare them with the plants growing in each location. Were your predictions correct? Remember that some plants may look quite different when they are young.

Plant adaptation

Plants grow in different **habitats** on almost every part of planet Earth. Although all plants need sunlight, air, water and minerals to grow, they have adapted so they can survive when any of these are in short supply.

Plant detective

Just looking at a plant can give you information about where it grows. Plants growing in dark woods often have tall stems to reach the sunlight. Mountain plants grow near the ground to protect themselves from cold winds. Desert plants store water in thick leaves or swollen stems.

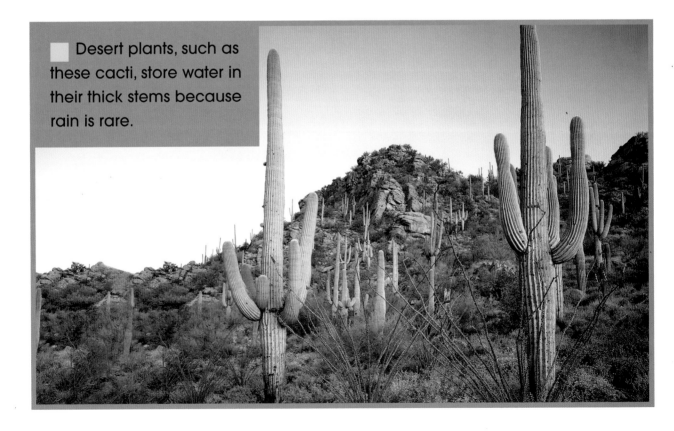

Desert plants, such as these cacti, store water in their thick stems because rain is rare.

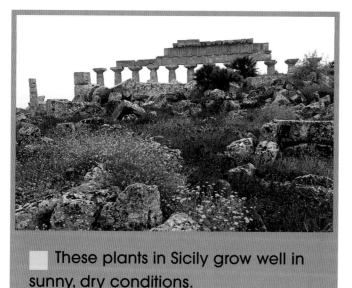

These plants in Sicily grow well in sunny, dry conditions.

Local plants

Plants that grow naturally where you live have adapted to the local conditions. Plants brought in from other habitats may not grow so well. For example, a plant from a sunny, dry area may not grow very well in a place that is often cloudy and wet.

Do a local plant survey

You will need:

- notebook • pencil and crayons • camera

1 Write a description of your local area and the green spaces found nearby. For example:

A built-up town, not many gardens, a big public park nearby, a school yard with a small patch of grass, hot, dry summers and cold, snowy winters.

2 Draw a table like the one shown opposite. Take photographs (or draw sketches) of plants growing near where you live. Write where they are growing and the date you recorded them.

Red geranium

Maple tree

Dandelion

Plant	Location	Date
Red geranium	Sunny porch	July
Maple tree	Outside our house	All year round
Dandelion	Front lawn	May

Why do you think the plants grow where you found them? Have they grown naturally or did someone plant them?

23

Plants for life

Plants provide most of the food eaten by people all over the world every day. Eating a variety of plants can give us the goodness we need to grow and to keep strong and healthy.

Food chain

A food chain shows how living things depend on each other for food. Plant-eating animals are called herbivores. Herbivores are food for meat-eating animals called carnivores. Animals who eat plants and meat are called omnivores.

In this food chain, plants make their food from sunlight, zebras eat plants, and lions eat zebras.

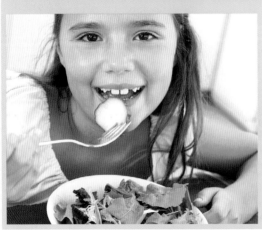

Eating a salad gives your body energy from plants.

Food plants

Most of the food you eat comes from plants or depends on plants. Bread and breakfast cereals are made from grain such as wheat, oats and rice. Chickens that provide us with meat and eggs are fed on grain. Cows that give us meat, milk and cheese eat grass and hay.

Discover food chains

You will need:
- large sheet of card
- pencils and crayons

1 Draw a chart, like the one shown here, onto the card.

2 Write down some of the food you eat in a day in the left column. Read the ingredients on the packet and look up the food in books or on the Internet to trace the food chain, starting with a plant and ending with you.

BREAKFAST	
Porridge	Oats/porridge -> me
Boiled egg	Corn -> chicken/egg -> me
LUNCH	
	Wheat/bread -> me
	Grass -> cow/butter -> me
Cheese sandwich	Grass -> cow/cheese -> me
	Lettuce -> me

How many food chains are you part of each day?

Caring for plants

We need to take care of plants. They keep the planet healthy by producing oxygen. Plants also provide us with food and important medicines that help us get better when we are ill. Many of the things people do put plants at risk.

Deforestation

Deforestation is the cutting down of forests to clear the ground for farmland or buildings. When trees are cut down and burned, carbon dioxide is sent into the air which traps heat from the Sun. This can contribute to **global warming** and **climate change**.

Cutting and burning trees is leading to rising temperatures on Earth.

These children are caring for plants in a gardening club.

What we can do

You can help to save the world's forests by using paper made from trees that will be replanted. You could also get involved in a scheme to protect a local green area or join your school gardening club.

Design a 'caring for plants' leaflet

What would you put in a leaflet asking people to care for plants?

For example:

Protecting plant habitats

- Buy paper and wood from forests that will be replanted.
- Support a local scheme that protects a plant habitat, such as a local wood or a park.

Out and about

- Don't pick or uproot plants without permission.
- Watch where you tread – don't squash plants!

Growing plants

- Grow plants that attract insects needed for pollination.
- Plant a tree or sponsor a tree.

Caring for plants

Don't tread on plants!

Water plants in your garden or your school garden.

If you don't have a garden, grow flowers and vegetables in pots and window boxes.

Glossary

adapt
To adapt is to change in order to survive in a particular place.

bulb
A bulb is a part of a plant that grows underground and stores food. A new plant grows from the bulb each year.

carbon dioxide
Carbon dioxide is a gas in the air that plants use to make food in their leaves.

chlorophyll
Chlorophyll is the green pigment in plants. It captures energy from sunlight to help plants grow.

climate change
Climate change is when the usual weather conditions in a place begin to change.

energy
Energy is the force that gives things the power to work. Energy gives plants the power to grow.

fruit
Fruit is the part of a plant that contains seeds.

germination
Germination is when a new plant starts to grow from a seed.

global warming
Global warming is the rise in the Earth's temperature. It is partly caused by too much carbon dioxide in the air.

habitats
Habitats are the natural surroundings of plants and animals.

minerals
Minerals are chemicals found in small amounts in the soil.

nectar
Nectar is a sweet juice made by plants in their flowers.

ovary
The ovary is the part of a plant where seeds are formed.

oxygen

Oxygen is a gas in the air that animals and plants need to breathe. Animals breathe in oxygen, plants release it.

photosynthesis

Photosynthesis is the way plants use chlorophyll, water, sunlight and carbon dioxide to make food in their leaves.

pigment

A pigment is a natural colour. Chlorophyll is the pigment that gives the stems and leaves of plants their green colour.

pollen

Pollen is the yellow powder made by the male part of a plant.

pollination

Pollination takes place in a plant when a pollen grain reaches the ovary, and seeds start to form.

seeds

Seeds are the parts of a plant that contain everything needed for a new plant to grow.

self-pollinated

A self-pollinated plant pollinates itself by moving pollen from its stamens to its pistil.

spores

Spores are a fine dust produced by plants that don't make seeds. A new plant grows from a spore.

tubers

Tubers are swollen roots or stems. They store food and form a new plant which grows.

water cycle

The water cycle is the way in which water goes round between the land, the sea and the air.

water vapour

Water vapour is formed when liquid water turns into a gas.

Index